WALKING THE MILFORD TRACK

The Experience of a Lifetime

D1785434

ROSALIND HARKER

Hodder Moa Beckett

ACKNOWLEDGEMENTS

The illustrations in this book were supplied by the following:

J.G. Blackwell
P. Bush
Department of Conservation
J.D. Harker
Z. Kepka
South Pacific Hotels Corporation

Special thanks to the Department of Conservation, Lake Te Anau, for their cooperation

ISBN 1-86958-796-0

First published in 1994 by
Moa Beckett Publishers Limited

Published by
Hodder Moa Beckett Publishers Limited
[a member of the Hodder Headline Group]
4 Whetu Place, Mairangi Bay
Auckland, New Zealand

Reprinted in 1996 (revised edition)
Reprinted in 1998, 1999, 2001, 2003

Typeset by Egan-Reid Ltd, Auckland

Printed in China through Bookbuilders.

PREFACE

. . . I especially feel the necessity of putting myself in communication with nature again, to recover my tone, to withdraw out of the wearying and unprofitable world of affairs . . . I wish again to participate in the serenity of nature, to share the happiness of the river and the woods.

– Henry David Thoreau

In the late seventies, my husband and I, faced with mid-career ennui, startled our friends by leaving our comfortable life on a Hawke's Bay farm to run Pompolona Hut on the Milford Track for the summer. One summer stretched to three, with much time to experience the track in all its moods and to explore it as only one living on it could. We have returned to it many times since with overseas nature lovers, who were as entranced with it as we were.

Although this book describes the Guided Walk, with which I am more familiar, the general advice I am giving on what one can expect to see, enjoy or endure, the preparation and the clothing to pack, is the same for both methods of walking the track.

Rosalind Harker

CONTENTS

THE MILFORD TRACK

AN INTRODUCTION

The Milford Track is a 55-kilometre (33-mile) dog-leg walk near the far northern edge of Fiordland National Park, which is the largest national park in New Zealand and part of the South-west New Zealand World Heritage Area. This area covers more than 1,213,574 hectares (3 million acres) and encompasses the south-west corner of the South Island.

Access to the track is by water, both at the beginning on Lake Te Anau and at the end at Milford Sound. In between, a four-day tramp follows the Clinton River up a U-shaped canyon sculpted by glacial ice, over a mainly granite mountain wall called Mackinnon Pass, and out to Milford Sound along the banks of the Arthur River and Lake Ada.

It is a walk of diverse beauty, characterised by lakes, rivers, waterfalls, snow-capped mountains, alpine flowers, ferns and mosses, beech and podocarp forests.

Many of the glaciers which have at times covered the area over the past two million years, shaping and gouging the valleys, are now lakes or fiords. There is no shortage of water. The westerly winds, heavy with moisture after travelling thousands of miles over unbroken sea, are forced to rise when they reach the Fiordland mountains, when the cooled air changes to heavy rain or snow. The annual rainfall in Milford Sound is 8,000 millimetres (320 inches), and at Te Anau 1,200 millimetres (48 inches). More than 200 days each year in Fiordland are wet, which contributes greatly to the scenery of waterfalls cascading down steep rocky faces, and of luxuriant rain forests encrusted with mosses, lichens and ferns.

ACCESS

Conditions, prices and arrangements for the Milford Track walk vary from season to season. The track usually opens in late October and closes in early April. It is closed in winter, when the sun is too low in the sky to reach the canyons, and very cold conditions prevail.

Children must be at least 10 years old as supervision can be difficult. People over 70 who are physically fit and in good health may be asked to produce evidence of this.

There are two ways to walk the track. One is the Milford Track Guided Walk, managed and marketed by the South Pacific Hotel Corporation. Tourism Milford, a company of which The Helicopter Line is part-owner, have the concession for the Guided Walk. It takes six days, although there is very little walking on days one and six, and walkers are in the care of a guide throughout the walk. Comfortable lodges are equipped with hot showers, drying rooms and bedding, and the walkers are well fed with farm-style meals.

Bookings for the Guided Walk are made with travel agents or at Milford Track Office, P. O. Box 185, Te Anau.

Variations on the six-day Guided Walk are available also. The Glade House Overnighter is designed for people who have neither the time nor the fitness to undertake the whole walk. It includes the trip up Lake Te Anau for a night at Glade House and part of a day exploring, and perhaps fishing, up the Clinton River valley, the beautiful beginning of the track, before returning in the late afternoon to Te Anau.

There is also a Partner's Package, in which a partner not walking the track can enjoy activities with track walkers at Te Anau and Milford Sound.

The Queenstown-Queenstown option, designed for those short of time, joins the Guided Walk on day two at Te Anau, and saves much of the last day by flying out of Milford Sound to Queenstown.

The other way to walk the Milford Track is by Independent Tramping using Department of Conservation huts (no camping is permitted in the park). This takes four days and three nights in well-appointed huts with gas cookers, drying rooms, and communal bunk-rooms with mattresses, basins, tables and benches. Independent walkers must carry their own food, cooking utensils and sleeping bags. Each hut has a staff member, with radio telephones for weather forecasts and in case of emergency. Reservations for Independent Tramping are made at the Fiordland National Park Visitor Centre.

FITNESS

There is so much to enjoy on the Milford Track that it is wise to be as fit as possible. Several months before the tramp, start tramping in the footwear you intend to use. Build up gradually until six hours' walking in a day does not leave you stiff or exhausted. There is no need to be masochistic, but forgo lifts, use stairs and walk up and down hills. Exercise off surplus body weight. Strengthen the legs by swimming, bicycling, playing golf or exercising, but remember, there is no substitute for walking when preparing for a walk. Though much of the track surface is even, in places it is rocky and uneven underfoot.

In fine weather, when you can dawdle, you might wonder why you were encouraged to undergo a fitness programme, but in bleak weather you realise why this is so important. The possibility of fording streams, being buffeted by strong winds or pelted by heavy rain necessitates being fit enough to move quickly in order to generate enough body heat to keep warm.

The track is not an easy walk, but neither is it difficult. People with limited disabilities manage it provided they are fit, healthy and sure-footed. With adequate preparation it is a walk of immense beauty and enjoyment, even in wet weather, when it is different but equally magical. Walkers are lucky if they experience both good and bad weather.

WHAT TO WEAR AND CARRY

The key word here is lightness. Bearing in mind that you carry your own pack, everything should be as light as possible. Very good parkas, bedsheets and raincoats are provided, but if you have a lighter, comfortable pack, use it. No pack is waterproof in Fiordland's downpours, so line it with a large plastic bag before packing. Similarly, the bed sheet provided must be sturdy to withstand constant laundering, but a silk or fine cotton one is lighter. Bring your own raincoat if it is waterproof in very heavy rain, and if it is light, and not so voluminous that it will billow out in strong winds.

The weather conditions can change quickly. Many people walk on four glorious, sunny days, others on four rainy days. You should be prepared for a mix of both.

A sunhat is necessary as the walk faces north, into the sun, much of the way. A woollen hat for cold weather is essential in an area where temperatures can drop dramatically. Choose wool or polypropylene garments for warmth, as they remain warm even when wet, and you will not feel chilled when you stop for a rest. More bulk does not necessarily mean warmth; weigh woollen garments and chose those that are light and warm. You will need a singlet, sweater, long johns, and a pair of socks, all of wool or polypropylene, and woollen gloves. Make sure the socks are soft wool, not harsh, as this makes a huge difference. I favour those with insides like terry towelling, with tiny loops of cushioning wool, that fit firmly on the calf to prevent small stones, kicked up into the back of the legs, falling down inside the heels of the socks and causing blisters.

Wear shorts over long johns and discard the latter on hot days. A cotton shirt should be carried for hot weather. Choice of boots is personal, but comfortable, light, well-broken-in boots with a good grip and a thick sole are ideal. No one needs to suffer blisters. Feet Fleece, a local wool product rich in lanolin, can be used inside socks to cushion the skin from friction. If, after all precautions, a blister does appear, a second-skin dressing reduces the discomfort miraculously.

For the evenings inside the huts a fine woollen jersey, light trousers or skirts are ideal. Featherweight footwear, worn with thin socks to foil the sandflies (which usually manage to infiltrate the huts to bite ankles) is all that is needed. The huts are warm, so summer pyjamas or T-shirt are adequate.

Save near-empty tubes of toiletries, or transfer small amounts into small plastic containers. The face and lips need protection from sun and wind, and all exposed skin needs insect repellent. During exertion noses usually run, so bring several cotton handkerchiefs.

Other items carried are a matter of choice. There are swimming opportunities for the brave. Some people like a small torch to use at night after the generator stops; others enjoy a pre-dinner drink and carry liquor in plastic containers. Fishermen will need current licences and rods, birdwatchers should bring binoculars. Bring some money or a credit card for optional flights or extra film at lodges. Do not bring towels, soap, shampoo or food.

Ideally your pack should weigh no more than 4.5 kilograms (10 lb) and preferably less. The lighter the pack, the greater will be your enjoyment.

THE GUIDED WALK

The Milford Track adventure begins at the township of Te Anau on the shores of Lake Te Anau, named after the granddaughter of a great Maori chief, Hekeia, who lived a thousand years before the white explorers arrived. C.J. Nairn, an explorer and one of the first Europeans to see Lake Te Anau, wrote in 1852, "The length of the lake I cannot guess, for it loses itself among the snowy mountains to the north." It was Mt Anau he saw, in the vicinity of the Track. The large blue gums on the shore feature in an early sketch of the township's site by D.C. Hutton in 1892, now in the Hocken Library in Dunedin. Lake Te Anau is New Zealand's second largest lake, with three large fiords lying to the north-west.

While in Te Anau, if time permits, a visit to Fiordland National Park Visitor Centre is well worth while – here are weather and track information, static displays of the flora, fauna and geology of the track and a short audio-visual on Fiordland National Park. A pleasant 15-minute walk along a path beside the Lake leads to the Wildlife Centre, where native birds may be seen. Many of these may be seen on the track, but not the takahe (*Notornis*), a large flightless, ponderous, brightly coloured bird of 63 centimetres (25 inches), previously thought extinct but rediscovered in the nearby Murchison Mountains by Dr G.B. Orbell in 1948.

Old historical photographs of the track are to be seen in the Turnbull Room at Te Anau Travelodge, where guided walkers usually stay their first night. At the hotel, prior to dinner, the preamble takes place in which walkers are briefed comprehensively on all aspects of the adventure. Packs and raincoats are distributed. Fears are allayed, advice is given, and the pattern of cheerful and good-natured shepherding is established. Fellow walkers are introduced over drinks, followed by dinner.

Next morning, after breakfast, check in at the Milford Track Office, after you have sorted out your luggage three ways. Firstly, luggage not required until you return to Te Anau and therefore stored at the Track Office. Secondly, a small bag of clean clothes you might like to wear on arrival at Milford Sound Hotel; the bag will be in your room there on arrival. Thirdly, your pack containing everything you need for the next four days and will carry over the track.

The rest of the morning is usually spent getting last-minute items, visiting Park Headquarters before lunch at the hotel, and having a group photograph outside the Milford Track Office. At one o'clock the bus leaves for Te Anau Downs.

2   TE ANAU → GLADE WHARF

BUS AND LAUNCH TRIP

On the bus ride from Te Anau to Te Anau Downs Harbour, walkers gain a taste of the bush to be seen later, as the bus passes through a clump of black beech (*Nothofagus solandri*) forest 17 kilometres (10 miles) out of Te Anau. Across the lake the entrance to the South and Middle Fiords can be seen. The use of the term 'fiord' (meaning a long, narrow arm of sea between cliffs) is not strictly accurate on Lake Te Anau, but Captain Hankinson, RN, who helped chart the lake, had been in Greenland's fiords.

Sudden changes of mood on the lake are caused by wind funnelling down the fiords. Just north from the entrance of the South Fiord is Garden Point, where Mackinnon, pioneer of the track, had his hut. Between the South and Middle Fiords glow-worm caves were discovered in 1946. These limestone caves, Te Ana-au Caves, are accessible by tourist launch from Te Anau. The Murchison Mountains, between the South and Middle Fiords, are the home of the takahe.

Track walkers leave the Milford Road at Te Anau Downs Harbour, where they board the MV *Tawera*. Flocks of a New Zealand scaup (black teal) are always seen here, small, dark, chunky birds swimming high in the water and diving for food. Little shags and black shags perch on the driftwood. In the old days wool was sent down the lake by boat from this sheltered little harbour. Its northern perimeter, named Welcome Point, must have promised sanctuary to many early sailors.

On leaving Te Anau Downs, the entrance to the North Fiord may be seen across the lake, while on the right is the entrance to the Eglinton River. Beyond the river on the right-hand side, and opposite the North Fiord, is the stone memorial to Mackinnon on Dot Island. Blue and pink lupins flower on the shore. They are not native plants, and are therefore unwelcome in the Park. Further on the cabbage tree (*Cordyline australis*) stands out along forest margins with its huge panicles of creamy white flowers.

While progressing up Lake Te Anau, one begins to see the result of Ice Age action, when huge glaciers of ice flowed off the mountains to scour the landscape westwards towards the sea and eastwards towards Central Otago, forming vertical-sided U-shaped valleys; above the ice, projecting mountain peaks were sharpened by severe frost action.

The wharf at Te Anau Downs

On the shores the dark colour of the beech forest is relieved by the lighter-coloured totara (*Podocarpus totara*), from which early Maori living here made their canoes, and rimu (*Dacrydium cupressinium*). Well up the lake Lee Island is passed, so named because shelter from winds can always be found on the side of this tiny island. It was used as a regular stopping place for Maori bringing greenstone from Milford Sound. During archaeological dating by Otago University in the early sixties, sticks, thought to have been used for fires, and greenstone were found here.

Beyond the North Fiord tree ferns are seen for the last time until near Quintin Hut. Here the lake narrows before opening out again, when the Worsley Valley is seen on the left. After going round a densely wooded promontory on the right, the end of the lake and Glade Wharf come into view. The wharf is near the right-hand side of the Clinton River, while on the left a shingle delta is seen – this was the landing place for the early steamers. Near here, high up on a ledge, was the first hut in the vicinity. Today, black-fronted terns enjoy the river mouth.

Before arrival at Glade Wharf, smother exposed skin with insect repellent. Captain Cook was right when he and his crew visited the Fiordland Coast in 1773; this much-travelled navigator wrote in his Journal:

> The most mischievous animals here are the small black sandflies which are very numerous, and so troublesome that they exceed everything of the kind I ever met with; wherever they bite they cause a swelling, and such intolerable itching, that it is not possible to refrain from scratching, which at last brings on ulcers like the smallpox.

Rata in flower, Lake Te Anau

3 GLADE WHARF → GLADE HOUSE

1 KILOMETRE

Coming off the wharf, one is immediately in beech forest. A large mountain beech (*Nothofagus solandri* var. *cliffortioides*) faces you with its small non-serrated leaves with rolled-down margins. In autumn a sweet smell may alert you to the presence of Easter orchid (*Earina autumnalis*) before the white flowers of this epiphytic, grass-like orchid are seen on this beech.

Beginning at the wharf, the entire track is marked with a sign after every mile. The track is wide and close to the Clinton River as far as Glade House, a distance of 1 kilometre. On the track edges look for hooded orchids (*Pterostylis banksii*). Ferns commonly seen along the track appear; crown fern (*Blechnum discolor*), its fronds erect and spreading to form a crown, and *Blechnum capense*, with its green, often reddish hanging fronds, but like all its genus having outer sterile fronds and an inner 'fruiting' frond which carries all the spores. This frond is often brown and appears dead.

Commonly hanging on the trees is hanging spleenwort (*Asplenium flaccidum*), a pendant epiphyte. The silvery bush flax (*Astelia fragrans*) is on the forest floor – the green gooseberry-like berries ripen to orange.

Meanwhile, the birds register your arrival. The bird making short darting flights across the track at head height ahead of you is likely to be the tomtit, with its black head and back and yellow breast – you will hear its high-pitched 'swee' the length of the track. It should not be confused with the native robin, which is larger, with dark-grey upper parts and creamy-white breast. The robin is fearless and inquisitive, and is likely to be standing long-legged and pert on the track, staring at you with beady eyes. The sweet trilling song will be that of the grey warbler, a small grey-brown bird with whitish belly. These birds usually move in pairs.

After passing through a clump of totara, the track opens up into a clearing once used for sheep pasture. Glade House, the guided walkers' first night's accommodation, stands here with some signs that it was once a homestead – an old pear tree out in front, lupins and wild strawberries in the grass. The Clinton River has a good fishing spot for rainbow trout – a bank of shingle and sand, just downstream

from The Glade. Further upstream there is access to swimming, near an isolated beech tree.

At Glade House the pattern for accommodation is established – comfortable beds, modern bathrooms, hearty meals, drying rooms. There is an atmosphere of fun and friendliness engendered by informative staff. Entertainment is the domain of the hutkeeper and his wife, but it usually takes the form of slide shows of the area ahead, and games to enable strangers to get to know each other. The guide may take the group for an energetic walk. If, when walking, you find

Glade Wharf at sunset

red flowers on the path, look up to find mistletoe (*Peraxilla tetrapetala*) growing parasitically on beech trees. On fine evenings, sunset over the lake at Glade Wharf is pretty, while after dark the Southern Cross may be seen over Skelmorlie Peak. Looking up the Clinton Valley from the verandas, one sees, looming large, a peak nicknamed The Sentinel. The Milford Track follows the valley on its left.

4 GLADE HOUSE → HIRERE FALLS

12 KILOMETRES

From Glade House, the track soon passes a small tree in the grass. It is mountain celery pine (*Phyllocladus alpinus*), which has tiny cones, and 'leaves', or cladodes, which are flattened stems, not true leaves. It, like totara and rimu, is a member of an ancient plant family, the podocarps, all conifers, which may be slowly declining and being replaced by beeches.

To the left in the Clinton River you will probably see paradise shelducks in pairs, the female with a conspicuous white head. Flying above them will be birds which feed on insects in flight – the fantail, acrobatic and lively, its tail fully spread when manoeuvring; also the chaffinch, the most common finch in New Zealand, introduced like all the finches, with white wing bars, and the male chestnut-breasted. The suspension bridge to cross the Clinton River is clearly visible long before you reach it, near where the One Mile peg (1.6km) should be, had a flood not claimed it. (For historic, practical and sentimental reasons the length of the track is marked in mile pegs, even though this country's system is now metric.)

Just before you step onto the bridge is a good example of an immature lancewood (*Pseudopanax crassifolius*) changing into its adult form. The lower leaves are long, narrow, leathery, sharp and serrated, drooping like the ribs of a partially-opened umbrella. On the top of the tree, the main stem branches are appearing with shorter upright leaves to form a canopy. A large flightless bird, the moa, now extinct, used to graze the forest margins. This change of form is thought to have evolved as a device against the moa's grazing, the young lancewood being unpalatable, the mature out of reach.

Crossing the bridge, black eels and rainbow trout of 2 to 4 kilograms (4–8 lb) can be seen in the clear water. Over the bridge the large trees ahead are silver beech (*Nothofagus menziesii*) with tall, straight trunks which are grey, rough and flaked when old, silver when young. The light green, dome-shaped serrated leaves are arranged in tiers on horizontally spreading branches. Sometimes silver beech are attacked by a pale yellow-orange, strawberry-like cup fungus (*Cyttaria gunnii*), which drops off onto the track like fruit. Also, here is red beech (*Nothofagus fusca*) with its larger, more serrated leaves which are reddish when young. The bark is then smoother and white, but when old is grey and deeply furrowed.

The track follows the banks of the snow-fed Clinton River. The water, because much of it has recently been snow, refracts light differently to produce an intense aquamarine colour on sunny days. About 600 metres (660 yards) from the bridge and perhaps 75 metres (80 yards) from where the track touches the river for the second time, there is a small cairn of stones on the left-hand side of the track. Leave your pack here and follow a narrow path for a few minutes to see a huge red beech. It is 10 metres (11 yards) in girth at shoulder height. Around its base grows giant moss (*Dendroligotrichum dendroides*) which looks like minute pine trees. Back on the track you will notice more red beech than silver – you will only see red beech between here and Pompolona Hut, then not again until near Milford Sound. Shortly you will see the site of Mackinnon's Two-Mile Hut on the left, which he built two miles from the lake where rocks prevented his taking a boat further. A small piece of iron from the original hut is nailed to a tree on a short loop track. Opposite is a stony beach suitable for fly

Clinton River

fishing. Some 200 metres (220 yards) on is the Two Mile (3km) peg, and the track continues without many bends until it passes signs of an old track claimed by the river in floods. This is Devil's Elbow, where successive floods have eroded the bank, forcing a track detour further back into the bush, in this case through a group of shrub-like pepper trees (*Pseudowintera colorata*), with leaves which are usually extensively blotched with red. If you pick up and crush a leaf or bite it carefully, you will understand why it is so named.

As the river curves, a sign points back to Dore Pass behind Glade House. The pass gives overland access to the track from the Eglinton Valley, but is only suitable for experienced mountaineers or trampers with a licence. It is high, and the track ill-defined. Behind you at the Dore Pass sign is more giant moss and, to the left of the sign, celery pine and totara. On the right of the sign is a mountain beech and a pale-lilac flowering koromiko (*Hebe salicifolia*). Like all hebes, it has leaves opposite each other in pairs, each pair being at right angles to the pairs above and below it. Just before the sign saying 'Neale Burn' are some old moss-covered totaras where the track touches the river again, one almost on the track on the right, and another opposite leaning towards the river.

At Neale Burn there is a lovely beach with a large rock to sit on, well worth a short detour. Across the river, where Neale Burn ('burn' being Gaelic for stream) runs in, is a turbulent area often favoured by the blue duck. These mountain ducks are occasionally seen in pairs over the first 18 kilometres. They are dove-grey with pinkish-white bills, adapted to feeding on aquatic insects by means of a rubbery lobe on each side of the bill. They feed on surface insects, but also enjoy diving in rough waters for insect life on stream beds. They are remarkably tame and have a characteristic whistling call. Before returning the few yards to the main track, you will see a kamahi (*Weinmannia racemosa*), a very common forest tree.

Soon you will see the sign to Clinton Forks Hut, where independent walkers spend their first night. Toilet facilities are available here.

Back on the main track, you climb the first small hill encountered to avoid an unstable river bank which often takes the full force of the river. By now you should have seen or heard the tui, or parson bird, a honeyeater. It is easily recognised as a black or iridescent green bird with white throat-tufts. Its fluid notes are interspersed with croaks, and will only be heard in several miles of bush at each end of the track, where it resides. Very similar in song is another honeyeater, the bellbird, the stronger notes of which sound bell-like from a distance. In colour it is soft olive-green, with a narrow tuft of yellow feathers on each side.

It is a slender and graceful bird, which enjoys feeding on honeydew produced by beech trees.

A rapid chattering call in the forest is made by the yellow-crowned parakeet, a bright green bird with a crimson forehead and yellow crown. The soft swish of wings and also wing flapping will help you find the New Zealand pigeon, a large, handsome, predominantly green bird with a prominent white breast – many other colours become evident when it is motionless and viewed closely.

Just past the Three Mile (5km) peg is a mountain beech with a steel hook embedded above head height. This was to hold a ceramic insulator for the telephone line, the only and unreliable means of communication between huts before radio contact. A straight stretch of track follows close to the river, then starts to undulate. New ferns appear as the track becomes cooler and wetter. Prince of Wales Feather fern (*Leptopteris superba*), much loved in the diet of deer, is easily recognised; it is very dark green, and the fronds are soft and feathery. Prickly shield fern (*Polystichum vestitum*) is also here; the frond's midrib and the rhizome from which it grows are densely covered with dark brown scales.

Shortly before the Four Mile (6.4km) peg is a footbridge; just before it, on the left, is a fuchsia tree (*Fuchsia excorticata*), the largest fuchsia in the world, common in second-growth areas, as here, along a stream bank. The purplish-red flowers, which hang downwards, become black, elongated berries favoured by pigeons, as evidenced by their purplish-black droppings. Fuchsia have a red, papery outer bark which peels to reveal smoother, yellow-green inner bark.

About here mica is seen shining like silver in the rocks on the track, while there is a good chance of seeing pairs of New Zealand's smallest native bird, a tiny wren called the rifleman. It spirals up tree trunks searching bark crevices for spiders and insects. Its tail is virtually absent; it is greenish-yellow, sometimes striped above, and white below. Its voice is as small as it is, and so high-pitched it is inaudible to some.

The track now leaves the river, so all is quiet again. The water in the side creeks is brown from tannins washed out of the ferns growing in them. Filmy fern (*Hymenophyllum multifidum*) appears on the tree trunks and mossy stones, almost transparent, as it is only one cell thick. After several hundred metres the track goes back to the river, and an expansive sandy beach perhaps 10 metres (9 yards) off the track. Fifty metres (55 yards) on is another sandy beach. Soon a sign indicates the Clinton River North Branch.

Looking up the North Branch into the distance, the Wick Mountains are sometimes visible. These mountains are close to Milford

A typical side creek

Sound, and on the last day of the walk walkers pass their base on the far side. Also up the North Branch, slightly to the right, Mt Anau can be admired.

A few metres from the North Branch sign is a small bridge, to the right and left of which are broadleaf trees (*Griselinia littoralis*) common in forests below 900 metres (3,000 feet) with their thick shiny leaves. The old track used to then plunge into the Black Forest, a stand of silver beech with tall, dark, twisted branches heavily festooned with mosses and lichens. But a recent flood once again forced a re-routing higher and deeper into the forest, so one looks down on the canopy. There are good stands of Prince of Wales Feather fern (*Leptopteris superba*) as you descend this re-routed track into the Black Forest. On the flat, still in the forest, is the Five Mile (8km) peg. Just opposite it is a five-finger (*Pseudopanax arboreus*), a common native tree which, despite its name, can have seven leaflets, as this one does.

Leaving Clinton Forks, the track now follows the west branch of the Clinton River past the Six Mile (10km) peg through forest, the floor of which is often thick with sphagnum moss (*Sphagnum cristatum*). On the edges of the track creeping pratia (*Pratia angulata*) forms tight mats; its tiny white flowers look as though some petals are missing. Look also for bog daisy (*Celmisia alpina*), minute white flowers arising singly on 7-centimetre (3-inch) stalks, and for the odd-leafed orchid (*Aporostylis bifolia*), a curious orchid in that, of its two leaves, one is much longer than the other.

On the left is the Castle Range, dominated by Mt Fisher, pointed and bare. This area has a history of avalanches, but a huge slip which came down in 1986 still scars the valley and must be scrambled over. *Trentepohlia*, a red algae, indicates the beginning of plant life on some rocks. The willowherb (*Epilobium glabellum*), with its red stems and green leaves, appears everywhere. Towards the end of the slip the Seven Mile peg (11km) is passed, from which there is a good view of the lake formed when this slip came down, and of the trees drowned in it. Colourful scabweeds form mats on the slip, binding the stones together and providing soil and humus for future plants.

Next comes a flat area and the original site of Six Mile Hut, which was abandoned because of the danger of avalanches. The nearby lake often has little shags perched on dead trees. The track winds along a narrow path through mountain holly (*Olearia ilicifolia*), small trees which have holly-like leaves, flat-topped racemes of white flowers and papery-thin peeling bark. Also in this area are two deciduous trees; wineberry (*Aristotelia serrata*) and mountain ribbonwood (*Hoheria glabrata*), which are some of the first trees to grow after slips. Wineberry flowers vary in colour, but are generally pale on opening and darken to pink with age; the deep red berries ripen to black. Mountain ribbonwood, commonly called lacebark because inner bark layers have a lace-like pattern, has pretty white, scented blossom. Flocks of silvereye, a small yellowish-green bird with a white eye ring, are often seen here enjoying the nectar and berries of these trees. A prickly liane, bush lawyer (*Rubus schmidelioides*), often forms a tangled mass over trees on the track, as it does here, and will hook onto anything brushing it. Its panicles of white flowers become red berries.

Just past the lake with its drowned trees the track comes back to the Clinton River again, with its aquamarine water and shingly beaches. Shortly the Hirere Falls Hut is reached, where guided walkers eat their lunch and meet the kea, a mischievous mountain parrot which is tame and playful. It will steal your lunch and shred anything left unattended. It is olive-green above with a scarlet underwing. Immature keas have yellow rings round their eyes; the older birds are more wily than the young. Across the canyon the Hirere Falls descends in leaps, while nearby a track leads to the river where rainbow trout may be seen; brown trout prefer to be closer to Lake Te Anau.

HIRERE FALLS → POMPOLONA

5 KILOMETRES

When you come back onto the main track again you will see a silver beech overhanging the track, festooned with filmy ferns and drooping spleenwort (already described) and also hound's tongue fern (*Phymatosorus diversifolius*), a very abundant fern. The fronds are thick and shiny, sometimes simple, like a hound's tongue, or many-leafed.

Shortly the Eight Mile (13km) peg is passed. In this area the river is shingle-bottomed, calm and quiet. Emerging out of the bush, weather permitting one gets the first view of Mackinnon Pass, Mt Hart on its left and Mt Balloon on its right. The first sight of the shelter hut, perched on the skyline of the Pass, has chilled the blood of many a walker. In fact, the gradient on the track up the Pass is no steeper than the occasional rise already encountered.

A glacier-flattened area follows. A side creek is crossed by bridge, after which a side loop-track leads walkers to the lake which feeds this creek – Hidden Lake. This is a good place for fly-fishing. However, in spring this loop track may be closed due to avalanche danger. Hidden Lake was gouged out by successive avalanches. High above it are rain-drenched snow-packs which feed the waterfall into it. Huge chunks drop off occasionally to form lakes or ice caves, while the air blast associated with the avalanche devastates the forest. Such activity is monitored, so obey the signs when you see a no-stopping zone; then you will be safe.

Just past where the Hidden Lake loop track rejoins the main track is a bank of clubmoss (*Lycopodium scariosum*), of ancient origin, with small leaves and cone-like structures called strobili on the tips of branches. Soon the track enters the bush again and follows the river, where there are some beautiful pools with trout and perhaps blue duck. The Nine Mile (15km) peg is passed, and another open area leads to Prairie Lake, nestled under Castle Range. It has a nice sandy beach, and if sunny the waterfall feeding it brings warmed water down the sun-heated side of the mountain, making it attractive for swimming. On its shores are clumps of a tall tussock (*Chionochloa conspicua*)

View of Mackinnon Pass and Mt Balloon

with large cream flower heads less dense than toetoe (*Cordateria richardii*), with which it is often confused. On the cliffs are large white mountain daisies (*Celmesia semicordata*). Their leaves appear silver underneath because of thick protective hairs.

The track now follows close to the left-hand side of the canyon, and passes through a grove of mountain holly. Curtains of dripping water or waterfalls run down to form small creeks which are stepped over between new tree avalanches. These have occurred when the weight of vegetation on steep areas cannot be supported by the thin layer of soil and interlocking roots, so the plant life slides off, denuding the rock face. At the end of a long, gently climbing hill, a substantial wooden shelter appears; this is called Bus Stop, and provides shelter when Marlene's Creek ahead, which is prone to flooding, is impassable. The flood waters drain away as quickly as they appear, but if in doubt wait for guides. The track is unclear over the creekbed full of boulders, but is marked upstream on the far bank by a large white 'T' nailed to a silver beech. A little more climbing, then the track goes downhill, to where there is a toilet facility on the right. The track then divides – the left branch leads to Mintaro and Mackinnon Pass; straight on leads to Pompolona Hut, the second night stop for guided walkers. The new Pompolona is a collection of connected modern chalets set in the bush, well away from the river, which destroyed old Pompolona.

At night you may hear the calls of the brown flightless kiwis, a shrill whistle of two notes, *ki-wi*. Being nocturnal and having poor eyesight, they will be out poking with their long bills on the forest floor for worms and insect larvae, or picking up ground insects. Another bird you might hear rather than see is the morepork, a small brown owl which calls *more-pork* intermittently. By day another flightless brown bird, the weka, is likely to walk across your path. Not at all shy, it is second only to the kea in its thieving habits.

6 POMPOLONA → PASS HUT

8 KILOMETRES

Leaving Pompolona, walkers must retrace their steps to the Pompolona/Mintaro turn-off and head towards Mintaro. The Eleven Mile (18km) peg is soon passed, and steep wooden steps lead down to the Pompolona Creek swing bridge. Looking upstream you will see the waterfalls feeding this creek, and possibly ice caves under the bluff. Looking back after crossing the bridge, a huge eroded shingly bank is all that is left of the old Pompolona site. Above, keas are often seen and heard flying up to the Pass hut, hoping to scavenge food.

Soon after leaving the creek, a small grassy clearing is seen to the left, all that remains of Stable Clearing, where the pack horses were fed and confined. One passes through areas devastated by successive avalanches, but with secondary growth of wineberry, lacebark, fuchsia and ferns. The redpoll, the smallest introduced finch, enjoys this area. It has a red forehead and the males have a pink breast. A sign indicates St Quintin Falls across the river, descending in three leaps from the ice field above.

A series of small footbridges take you over several small creeks in this open area near the Twelve Mile (19km) peg. In autumn the coprosma, hitherto nondescript shrubs, put on their display and become smothered with drupes (seeds surrounded by a fleshy coloured layer), here predominantly blue. On the grass verges several small flowers bloom: New Zealand bluebell (*Wahlenbergia albomarginata*) varies in colour from almost white to blue. The small white New Zealand violet (*Viola cunninghamii*) is found in damp places, while everlasting daisy (*Helichrysum bellidioides*) likes stoney places. The red seed heads of bidibidi (*Acaena novae-zelandiae*) attach themselves to the socks of passers-by.

The forest is re-entered as you climb the Mintaro Hill and pass the Thirteen Mile (21km) peg. The track and pools are often carpeted with lacebark flowers not unlike apple blossom. Shortly Lake Mintaro appears on the right, very sheltered, sequestered and limpid. As walkers pass it, the temperature is quite often rising, which lifts the mists lying in the canyon. This shows Lake Mintaro at its best, with mists rising through the primeval trees on its shores, perfectly reflected in the green water. Paradise duck, blue duck and Canada geese may be seen here.

A track up to the left leads to the Park Board's Mintaro Hut, the second night's stop for independent walkers. Toilet facilities for guided walkers are under the helicopter pad complex here.

After leaving Mintaro there is a side track down to a point for birdwatchers on the lake's edge. After skirting the lake and crossing the Clinton River by swing bridge, the Fourteen Mile (22km) peg is passed, and the wide zigzags up the Pass begin through bush and fallen trees heavily draped with moss and lichen. The second zigzag is very long, but at the end of it is a moss-covered fallen beech tree, an ideal seat for resting and removing your pack for a few minutes. Near the end of the third zigzag is a large rock; looking down past it is a fine view of Lake Mintaro.

On the sides of the track the bright yellow flowers of the Maori Onion plant (*Bulbinella gibbsii*) cover the top third of their stalks. This is also where you might see your first Mt Cook lily (*Ranunculus lyallii*), the world's largest ranunculus, whose white flowers appear after the snow melts, sometimes more than once a season. Its large, saucer-like leaf is unmistakable. The sight of acres of them flowering up the sides of Mt Balloon is unforgettable.

There is a steep angle onto the fourth zigzag, and the Fifteen Mile (24km) peg appears. Towards the end of it, on the left, is Haast's carrot (*Anistome haastii*), a deep green aromatic herb with carrot-like leaves and clusters of white flowers.

The fifth zigzag is short, but the sixth long, as one comes out of the tree line. Mountain daisies and bluebells abound, as do woolly heads (*Craspedia uniflora*), plants with woolly round flower-heads. Hebe shrubs bloom white; white snow marguerites (*Senecio scorzoneroides*) and yellow snow marguerites (*Senecio lyallii*) and their cream hybrids begin to appear in banks. To the left is the wide cirque at the head of the Clinton Valley; above it the Nicholas Peaks shed water from their snowfields to form the beginning of the Clinton River. To the left of Nicholas Peaks is Castle Mount, while they are flanked by Mt Hart on their right. Behind and hidden by Nicholas Peaks are the Sutherland Falls.

On zigzag seven Mt Balloon is straight ahead, and there is another good view of Lake Mintaro. On zigzag eight and onwards is *Forstera sedifolia*, a small herb which sends up a long, photosynthesizing stem, on the end of which is a small white flower to be pollinated. A tiny plant with creamy white, yellow-centred flowers is eyebright (*Euphrasia zelandica*), a root parasite which will be quietly sucking

Going up zig-zags on Mackinnon Pass

nutrients from the roots of its neighbours. Another herb found here is South Island mountain foxglove (*Ourisia macrocarpa*); its white flowers are arranged in whorls on stems up to 50 centimetres (20 inches) in height.

On zigzag nine look out for whipcord hebe (*Hebe laingii*), a low shrub up to 25 centimetres (10 inches) tall. The branches are almost square, and the leaves like overlapping scales for protection from the elements. Also look for midribbed snow tussock (*Chionochloa pallens*), distinguished by a midrib running the full length of the leaf. You will also have noticed a reddish spreading grass tree, pineapple scrub (*Dracophyllum menziesii*), a much-branched small shrub not unlike pineapple leaves.

As the summit of Mackinnon Pass is approached there is a stone cairn on the left, a memorial to Quintin Mackinnon erected by the Gaelic Society, the Otago Rugby Union and the New Zealand Government. From the edge of the cliff near the memorial is the most dramatic view on the track, made safe by a guard rail. Some 900 metres (3,000 feet) below, the Quintin huts and nearby airstrip can be seen in the Arthur Valley; the descent to these huts is made over the next 6–7 kilometres (4 miles). Standing at the cliff edge with Mt Hart on the left, one can see the next mountain beyond Mt Hart, which is Mt Mackenzie. Elizabeth Glacier, clearly seen on Mt Mackenzie, feeds Lake Quill, the source of water for the Sutherland Falls, so one can imagine where these famous falls are. Sometimes tourist planes disappearing in the same direction give a clue to their position also. Leaving Mt Mackenzie the eye passes over Staircase Valley to Mt Pillans, a large round mountain behind and dominating Quintin. Following the line of the airstrip, Green Valley leads the eye to Lady of the Snows at its head and rounded Dumpling Hill on the right, and beyond Dumpling Hill, Mt Edgar. Then, close by and to the right, comes Mt Elliot with its Jervois Glacier – this glacier is the last remnant of the great glacier which formed the Arthur Valley and Milford Sound. Along the right-hand side of the Pass, Mt Balloon rises steeply. You may see the track slanting down its left side, and turning under Mt Elliot back towards Quintin.

Near the cairn is a small tarn named Lake Stephen, after eight-month-old Stephen Cottle, who crossed the Pass many years ago in his father's pack. Always keep to the track. Do not take shortcuts and destroy delicate plants as you proceed along the Pass and pass the Sixteen Mile (26km) peg. On the banks a flattened shrub with white or red berries is the mountain snowberry (*Gaultheria depressa* var *novae-zealandiae*), and a daisy with sharp leaves, the dagger leaf daisy

Mackinnon Memorial, tarn and lookout on Mackinnon Pass

The Pass cloaked in mist.

(*Celmisia petriei*). There are various gentians here, all white (mostly *Gentiana montana*). An erect shrub reaching 1 metre (3 feet) with single white flowers is another grass tree, turpentine scrub (*Dracophyllum uniflorum*).

At the highest point, 1,154 metres (3,785 feet), there are fine views of Hidden Lake in the Clinton Valley and the huge slip scar behind it, as well as the pale bank at the old Pompolona site.

About 100 metres (110 yards) before Pass Hut, on the left and marked by a small stone cairn, is a patch of South Island edelweiss (*Leucogenes grandiceps*). If you miss it, ask the guide, as you are unlikely to see it elsewhere. The flower is made up of about 10 dense central yellow clusters, surrounded by a ring of up to 20 white woolly leaves. A small brown and white bird, spasmodically moving its tail up and down while walking and standing, is the pipit. More rare and half the size is the rock wren; it is almost tail-less, and is green above with yellowish sides. When feeding it flies a few yards, then lands with a curious bobbing action.

Pass Hut, well tied down against the elements, is a lunch shelter used by guided walkers and independent walkers, each with their own facilities and rooms. Outside, there is a toilet facility with a much-talked-about view of the Clinton Valley. Keas frequent the Pass Hut area hopeful of being fed. Please do not feed them, as this makes it difficult for them to fend for themselves in winter; just enjoy their amusing antics.

On the rocks near the hut grow two plants flat enough to escape winter winds, and dense enough to prevent others getting a foothold. The cushion plant (*Phyllachne colensoi*), a very ancient plant, survived the ice-age by its form. Often on its own part of the same rock is one of New Zealand's famed vegetable sheep (*Raoulia eximia*), so called because from a distance its pale round shape has been mistaken for a sheep. Both these plants densely hug the rocks they grow on, conserving moisture. The mat of the much less dense cushion daisy (*Celmisia sessiflora*) grows amongst the grasses with rosettes of overlapping leaves.

Clinton Valley from Mackinnon Pass

Jervois Glacier on Mt Elliot, viewed across tarns

PASS HUT → QUINTIN

7.4 KILOMETRES

There is a general agreement that the descent to Quintin is the toughest part of the track, as it is downhill, rocky and uneven underfoot, and 900 metres (3,000 feet) is descended in 6–7 kilometres (4 miles). The route goes round the side of Mt Balloon past the Seventeen Mile (27km) peg, through tussock.

Although the vegetation is similar to that already seen going up the Pass, new species appear, such as large-flowered native broom (*Carmichaelia grandiflora*) with its purple and white sweet-smelling flowers. Also found here is Fiordland spaniard (*Aciphylla takahea*), a speargrass found only in Fiordland, with dagger-like leaves and a tall, spiked, yellow flower head.

The track begins a series of short zigzags descending to a grassy spur, then leads off under the bluffs again. A sign indicates the Emergency Track, which is used if there is avalanche danger ahead on the main track, especially in spring. It will be quite clear which track to use, as the other one will be blocked off. Near the junction mountain flax (*Phormium cookianum*) grows, a tall plant with sword-like, pale green leaves and yellowish flowers.

The descent is steeper on the Emergency Track. Two creeks are crossed, Moraine Creek and Roaring Burn. After Dudleigh Falls are passed, one rejoins the main track about 1 kilometre before Quintin. If the main track is used, continue on this easier route. Look out for a new grasstree (*Dracophyllum fiordense*), a small tree up to 3 metres (10 feet) in height, with one trunk and one or two branches with dense clusters of leathery leaves at their ends. Moraine Creek is crossed and the avalanche area is entered with everlasting daisies, willowherbs, bidibidi and scabweeds appearing. As the ice of the Jervois Glacier above shrinks, snow is more likely to slide off bare rock than off glacial ice, causing avalanches. As with other avalanche areas, this area is monitored for safety.

Soon a sign indicates the first view of the Sutherland Falls top leap. Lacebarks appear, as do waxeyes, and possibly noisy flocks of brown creepers, reddish-brown birds with pale cinnamon underparts. Pairs of yellowhead, a bush canary, are easily recognised feeding on the tops of trees. The Eighteen Mile (29km) peg is passed as well as a working

Descending under Mt Balloon

building, Crows Nest. Patches of a grey-green shrub, with a musky smell, seen in this area are musky tree daisy (*Olearia moschata*).

Roaring Burn is crossed by stone hopping or by bridge if necessary. There are various small side creeks and grottos on the side of Mt Elliot. As you re-enter the beech forest, watch for the mountain cabbage tree (*Cordyline indivisa*) growing in open places where there is plenty of light. It may be 6 metres (19 feet) tall, and has a single trunk topped by a huge tuft of sword-shaped leaves.

As Quintin is approached the last kilometre descends steeply. Dudleigh and Lyndsay Falls are glimpsed and heard in Roaring Burn's downward path. Suddenly, and to the intense relief of many, a sign appears at a T-junction. Take the track to the left to Quintin Huts, the third overnight stop for guided walkers and the site of a shelter hut for independent walkers, who leave packs here on the side excursion to Sutherland Falls.

SUTHERLAND FALLS

8

4 KILOMETRES RETURN

During the stopover at Quintin Huts, it is well worth overcoming any physical reluctance to cover the extra 2½ miles (4km) to the Sutherland Falls and back, which takes an hour and a half. (If the body and spirit are unwilling there is a good view of them from the main track after leaving Quintin.)

Near the beginning of the track to the Falls are soft tree ferns (*Cyathea smithii*), with large pointed fronds and a 'skirt' of dead leaf stems around the trunk below the new leaves. Filmy ferns grow on a

Approaching Sutherland Falls

large kamahi overhanging the track some 100 metres (110 yards) along. Hen and chicken ferns (*Asplenium bulbiferum*) appear, with small plants (the 'chickens') growing on the outer edges of the fronds. Hound's tongue fern hangs down from the first tree arched over the track. On the verge edges, just before the bridge over the Arthur River, are leafy patches of native oxalis (*Oxalis lactea*) with very small white flowers. Quite a steep hill is climbed, and just before the track flattens out are some fine specimens of Prince of Wales Feather ferns. Sutherland Falls are now heard, and shortly the top leap, then the second leap can be seen. A notice soon announces 580 metres (1,904 feet) to the falls, the same distance as their height.

Shortly the three leaps are seen (and felt). After heavy rain the three leaps become almost indistinguishable due to the huge volume of water thundering down, creating whirlwinds which shoot spray in all directions. Drumming, swishing and rasping sounds are all intermingled as the walker is greeted by misty rain near the falls. C.W. Adams, the early surveyor, lecturing on the falls to Australians, said, "If it had been my fortunate lot to have discovered these falls I should not have given them my own name; but called them the Rainbow Falls." He was referring to the sight of them in the morning, the best time to see them, when sunbeams make rainbows in the mists.

The lowest leap lands in a pool at the base, pounding a rock in the middle. If the weight of water is sufficient to project it well out, one can go behind the falls from the left – an exhilarating, though wet and noisy experience. When the volume of water is not great, each leap of the falls is distinct, and one can stand at the edge of the pool, barely getting wet. If the wind is blowing, the falling cataract swings in the winds, sometimes exposing the flat rock in the pool and thus varying the sounds produced.

This is, indeed, an enchanting place. Mountain daisies, cabbage trees and flax, marguerites, woolly heads and sometimes scarlet-flowering rata (*Metrosideros umbellata*) frame the falls. The three giant leaps can be seen, the top leap of 248 metres (815 feet), the middle leap of 229 metres (751 feet), and the lower leap of 103 metres (338 feet) totalling in all 580 metres (1,904 feet), the fifth highest waterfall in the world.

Weather permitting, scenic flights are available from the airstrip at Quintin. The planes fly over the Sutherland Falls and Lake Quill, which feeds them, into the Clinton Valley, over Mackinnon Pass and back to Quintin. Wonderful views of the mountains, glaciers and lakes, often unseen while walking, put the walk into perspective.

9

QUINTIN → SANDFLY POINT

22 KILOMETRES

Leaving Quintin, there is a stone cairn on the grass by the front door of the lodge. On its shady side hound's tongue ferns grow. High up on the large beech tree between the bunkrooms, orchids may be seen or smelled. Cross the bridge back to the sign that reads 'Sandfly Point – 7 hours'. About eight strides past the sign, look on the right bank near the ground for the aerial stems of the chain fern (*Tmesipteris elongata*). Its leaves, about 2 centimetres in length, are arranged in spirals along its pendulous stems, the end ones being divided into two and bearing spores. Look, but do not touch. These are rare and ancient plants.

The track passes the Twenty Mile (30km) peg and runs parallel to the airstrip, past regenerating avalanche areas. Towards the end of the airstrip the two top leaps of Sutherland Falls are seen beyond it. In the near foreground is toetoe (*Cordateria richardii*), not unlike pampas grass, and tutu (*Coriaria arborea*), a stout shrub with racemes of tiny cream flowers and black berries, which are poisonous. Shortly, all leaps of the falls are seen for the last time. The bank here is covered with mosses and lichens.

You may come across two harsh-calling birds in this area. The kaka, a parrot heard calling in flight, is distinguishable from the kea on landing by a greyish-white crown and more red on its abdomen. The long-tailed cuckoo is more often heard than seen; it has a harsh, piercing, long-drawn-out screech. Brown above and white underneath, spotted and streaked, it has a very long tail.

When you cross the first dog-leg-shaped bridge, look to both sides of the bridge for palmleaf fern (*Blechnum capense* 'blackspot'), which has very long fronds hanging down, up to 360 centimetres (142 inches). On the right at the end of the bridge is an astelia. There follows a grove of crown ferns on the left, and soon the long downhill rocky slope called Gentle Annie begins.

As you pass the Twenty-one Mile (33.5km) peg you will see rough tree ferns (*Dicksonia squarrosa*). They have no 'skirt', but their trunks are dark brown due to persistent leaf stems which remain after the leaf has broken off. A clearing then gives a view of Dumpling Hill and Mt Edgar, and a peep of Lady of the Snows on the left.

The track undulates past old avalanche areas until it descends through a steep cutting onto Sandy Flat, which is prone to flooding. A 175-metre (180-yard) bridge winding under the bank leads to Dumpling Hut, the third night's stop for independent walkers, where toilet facilities are available.

The Twenty-two Mile (35km) peg is passed, and soon silver beech forest is entered. Types of trees seen earlier appear again, but are more lush because of the higher rainfall and milder temperature in the Arthur Valley. As the river gets closer, a regeneration area of fuchsia, pepper tree, broadleaf, tutu and bush lawyer includes a long level section known as Racecourse Flat, where in the 1930s the pack horses vied with each other to take the lead. With views of Mt Kepka on the right, the Twenty-three Mile (37km) peg and Twenty-four Mile (38.5km) pegs are passed; just before the latter are Prince of Wales Feather ferns.

Passing between large rock pillars, Boatshed is reached. A boat used on Lake Ada for ferrying heavy luggage, or for carrying people across the river, used to be housed here. Now it is a refreshment stop for guided walkers. Toilet facilities are here. A beautiful pool in the river below the hut is popular for swimming.

From Boatshed there is a fishing option at extra cost for guided walkers in limited numbers. They are taken down the Arthur River into Lake Ada, formed a thousand years ago when rock falls and landslides dammed the river, drowning the forest, the tree stumps of which may still be seen when the lake level is low. Brown trout are here in abundance, and one can fish from either the boat or the shore. It is a beautiful, pristine, lonely area, but those who choose this option will miss walking over 9.5 kilometres (six miles) of the track, which they join at Doughboy, well down the lake.

Leaving Boatshed, walkers cross the Arthur River to its northern bank by a suspension bridge which is high enough to survive in this flood-prone area. There follows an area of ribbonwood, and its flowers carpet the forest floor. In this flat area, made easier by boardwalks, glance up the mountain sides for the crimson flowers of the rata tree. When it is flowering profusely in the valley, one can see a line above which it does not grow.

The Twenty-six Mile (42km) peg is followed by the Mackay Creek swing bridge. Shortly, leaving one's pack, one may visit the beautiful Mackay Falls and Bell Rock on a side track. Mackay Falls are within sight of Bell Rock. Some 3 metres (10 feet) in height, this rock may be crawled under to reveal, on striking a match or shining a torch, a hollow large enough for three people to stand upright. Water

Swing bridge over Arthur River at Boatshed

and stones originally eroded it over the centuries in the creekbed, before it rolled down the hill to rest upside-down on the bank of the creek.

The forest continues until an open area of lower ground is reached, subject to flooding from the river and slips from the steep hillside. A series of boardwalks considerably aid walking here. The Twenty-seven Mile (43.5km) peg is in this area. Dense forest is entered again, with red beech appearing in greater numbers. Poseidon Creek, spanned by a suspension bridge, and the Twenty-eight Mile (45km) peg are passed, and within 2 kilometres Lake Ada comes into view. Here paradise and grey duck, grey teal, black shags and swans may be seen.

The track around the edge of Lake Ada is blasted out of the perpendicular rock wall. There are fine views from it – the Wick Mountains across the lake are the ones already seen up the North Branch of the Clinton River; they were named by Donald Sutherland after his birthplace in Scotland. The entrance to Joes River, where Sutherland and Mackay looked in vain for a pass to the interior, precedes the Wick Mountains and Mt Sheerdown, nearer Milford.

On the wall of the cutting, near the top, look for lady's slipper or tree orchid (*Dendrobium cunninghamii*) which, despite its name, will grow on rocks. As the rock walk descends from the Twenty-nine Mile

MacKay Falls

Giant's Gate Falls

(46.5km) peg, some way down, on the right, kidney fern (*Cardiomanes reniforme*) appears for the first time, a filmy fern easily distinguished by its kidney-shaped fronds. They are seen again growing in dense mats on rocks and banks right down to sea level.

At the Thirty Mile (48km) peg it is possible to hear Giant's Gate Falls, which are approached over a bridge, before which a shelter for all walkers is available. There is a lovely picnic spot on the rocks across the bridge. Giant's Gate Falls are passed with less than 5 kilometres (3 miles) to go. It seems a long stretch past the Thirty-one Mile peg (49.5km) to the next hut, Doughboy, at the end of the lake, as the going is flat and the views unvaried. Doughboy was the launching place for the boat ferrying supplies up Lake Ada. Take a short walk out onto the wharf here to view the lake.

From there to Sandfly Point the track is wide, a relic of the days of tractor and trailer. Many of the plants and trees here you will have seen at the beginning of the track, such as the sweet-smelling orchids and the mosses; but some will be new or previously missed, such as marble-leaf (*Carpodetus serratus*), with mottled leaves. There is a marble-leaf tree past the Thirty-two Mile (51.5km) peg at the far left-hand end of the steel bridge which crosses over Camp Oven Creek. A fine-leafed, dense creeper climbing up tree trunks, flowering white high up, is the white rata (*Metrosideros diffusa*).

Some mature conifers appear, both podocarps. Rimu (*Dacrydium cupressinium*), a tall straight tree with grey, thick, flaky bark, has a charming juvenile form with light green pendulous leaves. Miro (*Prumnopitys ferruginea*) is a tree of similar size to the rimu, its juvenile form graceful and also pendulous, and its leaves soft to touch. Its large red seeds, which have a purple bloom when ripe, are well-liked by the native wood pigeon, which plays a large part in their seed dispersal.

At the Thirty-three Mile (53km) peg there is roughly a kilometre of the track to complete close to the river.

Soon the Tasman Sea comes into view at the infamous Sandfly Point, not a place to linger unless one has a good supply of dimethylphthalate. Maori legend has it that Hine-nui-te-po, the Goddess of Death, visited the god Tu-to-Rakiwhanoa at Sandfly Point as he carved out Milford Sound. She found it so beautiful she feared mortals would want to linger there forever, so she liberated a large species of namu, or sandfly, with an injunction that they multiply – and multiply they did. Fortunately, there are closed shelters in which to await the launches at two, three and lastly four o'clock.

The boat passes a flat promontory on the right, covered with rimu and rata with a margin of toetoe. Behind it Sheerdown Mountain towers; beyond its base, a tree and rock avalanche scar marks the position of the road one takes out of Milford Sound up the Cleddan Valley to the Homer Tunnel and on to Te Anau. Further into the Sound, past the fishing fleet's anchorage, is the airstrip; flying is the alternative means of leaving Milford Sound, weather permitting. But that is tomorrow. Bus transport at the wharf awaits to ferry you to your hotel, where a mixture of emotions take over. Relief, pride and gratitude are mixed with a sense of achievement and refreshment of the spirit. Celebrations are more than deserved.

10

MILFORD SOUND

Next morning, a Milford Sound cruise is a stunning finale, with the added bonus of no physical effort. The route taken is usually down the left-hand side of the fiord below Mitre Peak, rising 1,692 metres (5,560 feet) above sea level with another 305 metres (1,000 feet) below water. Its sides, clothed in beech, kamahi and rata, have rock faces coloured in parts by copper and iron oxides. Waterfalls pour into the sound, some permanent, others after rain, gathering brown tannin from tree roots on the way to produce a layer of brown water 2 metres (6 feet) thick floating on top of the seawater, and excluding much light. This allows corals, sponges and other sea creatures to live much nearer the surface than normally.

Milford Sound — Mitre Peak on left, The Elephant and The Lion in the middle, Mt Pembroke on the right.

On the rocks Southern seals bask, while in the Sound bottle-nosed dolphins disport themselves around the boat's bows. Penguins swimming are easily identified by two yellow crests on their heads as Fiordland crested penguins. On the homeward journey look out for them on the shoreline.

Before the fiord entrance is Anita Bay, where Maori sought valuable greenstone (a nephrite jade) years ago. A sortie out into the Tasman Sea to see the rugged coastline follows. The return cruise goes along the other side of the fiord below towering cliffs, still showing the scars of the glaciers which shaped them, and mountains affectionately called The Lion and The Elephant. From Harrison Cove, the only natural anchorage in the fiord, there is a fine view of Mt Pembroke and its glacier which, like Jervois Glacier on Mt Elliott, helped shape Milford Sound. A solitary white heron is sometimes standing or perching at low tide near the wharf. This lone, beautiful bird seems to embody the beauty of the scenery here.

If time permits, a 15-minute return walk from the wharf to the Bowen Falls is a delight. The boardwalk follows the coastline against a dripping bank, covered with mosses and ferns. Of special interest, growing out of the moss, is the small carnivorous sundew (*Drosera arcturi*), which catches insects in sticky red hairs on its leaves, then absorbs and digests them. Much of the vegetation approaching the falls will be familiar from the track, but easier to observe.

Following lunch most walkers return to Te Anau by bus through towering glaciated mountains and forests. As Lake Te Anau comes into view, where the launch was boarded four days previously, spare a thought from the comfort of the bus for those track-walkers who before 1940 could not return by road tunnel, but instead walked the track in reverse. Yet by the time the bus arrives at Te Anau township those earlier walkers might be envied, as one remembers the beauties of the Milford Track, different but no less beautiful when walked in the opposite direction.

11   HISTORY OF THE TRACK

In the names of places along the Milford Track are many echoes from the past. Mountains, lakes, waterfalls and passes often bear the names of those who pioneered this rugged region.

In pre-European times, Maori in Fiordland largely confined themselves to Milford South, where they hunted for waterfowl and collected greenstone, or nephrite. This highly prized stone was laboriously shaped with abrasives such as sand to make weapons, tools and ornaments. Greenstone was transported along a route much like that of the track today, but with more use of waterways.

A man whose name is intrinsically bound up with the history of the Milford Track is Donald Sutherland. He was born in the north of Scotland in 1840. His love of adventure and the sea brought him to New Zealand, where he took part in the Gabriel's Gully gold rush and also gained mining experience on the Coromandel Peninsula and West Coast of the South Island. During the New Zealand wars of the 1860s he enlisted as a militiaman, but once the wars were over returned to the sea to serve on the government steamer *Stella*.

From that ship Donald Sutherland first saw Milford Sound. His rather limited mining experience led him to believe there was immense mineral wealth in the surrounding area – gold, diamonds, rubies, greenstone and asbestos – for which he later prospected. He first landed at Milford Sound on 1 December, 1877. Seeing signs of 'natives' he cautiously camped on an island in the Arthur River. He went up-river and named Lake Ada, then returned to explore Freshwater Basin.

In 1888 C. W. Adams, Chief Surveyor of Otago, commissioned Sutherland, with the reward of £50, to cut a track, the forerunner of the Milford Track, from Milford South to the Sutherland Falls. This feat was accomplished in six months with the help of three assistants. It was Adams' aim to find an overland track to Te Anau.

At the same time Quintin Mackinnon was commissioned by Adams, for £30, to blaze a track up the Clinton Valley from the head of Lake Te Anau. In September 1888, therefore, the overland route between Te Anau and Milford was being sought from both ends.

Quintin Mackinnon came from the Shetland Islands, were he was born in 1851, the son of a Presbyterian minister. As a young man he had fought for the French in the Franco-Prussian War. By the 1870s he was in New Zealand playing rugby for Otago. At 30 years of age, in 1881, he qualified as a surveyor and made his home at Garden Point on the shores of Lake Te Anau. He was a small, powerful man with a ready wit, who rejoiced in the nickname of Rob Roy.

On 2 September, 1888, Ernest Mitchell, of Manapouri Station, and Quintin Mackinnon left Te Anau in a sailing boat for the head of the lake and the Clinton Valley. After a night at Lynwood Station and two at Te Anau Downs they sailed on, laden with provisions, tools and tents. A mile up the Clinton River they set up a camp, having left some reserve provisions and a tent by the lakeside.

On 17 September they started to cut the track, marking trees as they went. Drenched by rain, both inside their tent and out, they were beleaguered by sores, cold and hunger. As they were unable to light a fire, cooking food or making hot drinks were impossible – nor could they dry out their bedding or clothes. At one stage food was so short they had to ration themselves to one meal a day. After three weeks of hard work in unpleasant conditions, they were nine miles up the Clinton Valley.

After a few more days cutting in pouring rain they abandoned their tools and went ahead to reconnoitre the area, and discovered Lake Mintaro. Pushing on, they hauled themselves to the top of the Pass, using any foothold or handhold they could, until they stood on top. It was 16 October, 1888.

Hampered by poor visibility and driving rain they groped around for a way down the other side, which they found at the base of Mt Balloon. Halfway down they found shelter of a sort, so turned in for the night, soaking wet and supperless.

Next day, still descending, they came to a shingle beach at two o'clock in the afternoon. Here they found dry firewood, boiled a billy and grilled a blue mountain duck. Later on the same day they intercepted Donald Sutherland's track, left a message and went on to Lake Ada.

On arrival at Milford, Mackinnon wrote in Sutherland's visitors' book, "Found good available track from Te Anau to connect with Sutherland's track at Beech Hut. Found Government maps very much out and the Hermit's very much in."

The Hermit was Sutherland who, despite this piece of flattery, was peeved that Mackinnon had found the route he had sought for eight years.

The day following Mackinnon and Mitchell's arrival at Milford,

Quintin Mackinnon (centre) with companions. Note the kakapo perched on the pole.

Mackinnon and three others, including Muir, a photographer, set off on what was to be the first crossing of the Pass from north to south. They approached the Pass straight upwards, but were thwarted about two in the afternoon by a smooth, overhanging rock that was impossible to climb. They retreated a short distance and camped overnight in view of the Jervois Glacier, which they named for the Governor of New Zealand at the time.

Next day they found a route over the Pass in a snowstorm, and found their way to the shelter of the Clinton Valley. There was not much respite from the elements there, as they had to wade the icy river. The following day they reached Lake Te Anau. In an account Mackenzie wrote for the *Otago Daily Times* he mentions clematis festooning the beech trees near the lake, and numerous birds including the kakapo, the moss-green parrot – alas, not seen on the Track today. Muir took the historic photo of Mackinnon pointing to the pass that bears his name and his memorial.

The four men sailed down a very rough lake in their anxiety to tell the country they had found the long-sought-for route to Milford. It was Mackinnon's privilege to send this news in a telegram to the government from the township of Lumsden.

The government, recognising tourist potential, now decided to develop the route by upgrading the track and the huts. At Milford Sound, Sutherland and his wife built a 12-roomed house to accommodate people coming either by sea or over the Pass. Called 'The City of Milford', it was used until 1919 when Sutherland died. A huge man, he fell out of his bed onto the floor where his wife, unable to lift him or summon help, nursed him until he died. He was buried six weeks later when the *SS Hinemoa* arrived.

Mackinnon, the first official guide on the track, lived at Garden Point at the entrance to the south arm of Lake Te Anau. His parties left Te Anau in his whaleboat, *Juliet*, in which they travelled to the head of the lake.

At his canvas camp at Pompolona he produced his culinary speciality, pompolonas, a type of scone fried in mutton fat or melted candles. He eventually met his death by drowning in Lake Te Anau. It was his habit to sit at the stern of the boat at the tiller and it was thought he had been knocked overboard.

In 1908 the track received some unexpected publicity when the *Spectator* (London) published an article on it called *The Finest Walk in the World*, a title which has lasted to this day.

In 1964 a group from the Otago Tramping Club walked the track to demonstrate that anyone had the right and ability to use it, and to challenge what they saw as the Tourist Hotel Corporation's monopoly. These 'Freedom Walkers', after experiencing rain and a high-running Arthur River, conceded that help and guidance were needed for some trampers. The Fiordland Park Board therefore built a series of huts at strategic intervals along the track for 'Independent Walkers'.

But perhaps the biggest event to affect walkers of the Milford Track was the development of the Milford Road between Te Anau and Milford. During the Depression the Government used unemployed labour for road-building in remote areas. Men armed with shovels, picks and wheelbarrows began building the 30-kilometre (19-mile) road from Te Anau to Te Anau Downs Station in 1929, later penetrating further into the Eglinton Valley. By 1934 it had reached the Divide between the Eglinton and Hollyford Valleys, where the road was taken steeply down into the Hollyford Canyon and to the Marian construction camp.

Some 14 kilometres (9 miles) up the Hollyford Canyon is the Homer Saddle, discovered and named by W. H. Homer in 1889. Homer was most enthusiastic about boring a tunnel through to the Cleddau Canyon, but whereas a surveyor once declared it feasible for £2,000, it became a reality nearly 50 years later at a cost of over half a million pounds.

ERECTED
BY THE GAELIC SOCIETY OF N.Z. AND
THE OTAGO RUGBY FOOTBALL UNION
ASSISTED BY THE GOVERNMENT

IN HONOUR OF

QUINTIN MACKINNON
EXPLORER

WHO DISCOVERED THIS PASS IN 1888 AND
WHO IN 1892 WAS DROWNED IN LAKE TE ANAU

HON. T. MACKENZIE, F.R.G.S., PRIME MINISTER.
HON. W.D.S. MACDONALD, MINISTER OF PUBLIC W.
DUGALD McPHERSON, CHIEF OF GAELIC SOC.

THIS PLAQUE COMMEMORATES THE 100th
ANNIVERSARY OF THE DISCOVERY OF THE PASS
BY QUINTIN MacKINNON AND ERNEST MITCHELL

ERECTED BY THE TOURIST HOTEL CORPORATION
OF NEW ZEALAND AND DEPARTMENT OF CONSERVATION
ON OCTOBER 16 1988 AS PART OF THE
MILFORD TRACK CENTENNIAL
CELEBRATIONS

In 1935 five men started excavating the tunnel with picks and shovels and wheelbarrows. A year later they had passed through the outer scree and began penetrating the solid rock by blasting with explosives, which possibly activated avalanches. The tunnel entrance was right in the path of avalanches from a snowfield above on the Saddle. After one tunneller was killed in midwinter, 1936, by an avalanche, a covered way was built out from the entrance. This did not prevent the deaths by avalanche blast in 1937 of D. F. Hulse, the engineer, and T. W. Smith, the overseer.

The work was dangerous and uncomfortable, with avalanches, snow, sleet, rain and sandflies to contend with. At first the men lived in tents, later replaced by permanent huts. Despite the hardships, in March 1940 the Milford side was pierced. The tunnel is 1 kilometre in length. It enters on the Hollyford side at 976 metres (3,203 feet) above sea level and emerges on the Milford side 792 metres (2,600 feet) above sea level. With the opening of the tunnel and the road right through to Milford, the round trip for walkers via the tunnel could be made.

Maintaining the track and its facilities was and still is, an endless task. Fire, flood, wind and avalanche have all taken their toll over the years. Helicopters have replaced packhorses and tractors, modern huts have taken the place of tents, but the track itself remains much the same, ever at the mercy of the elements.

12 FLORA OF THE TRACK

Bidibidi *(Acaena novae-zelandiae)*
Black beech *(Nothofagus solandri)*
Bog daisy *(Celmisia alpina)*
Broadleaf *(Griselinia littoralis)*
Bush flax *(Astelia fragrans)*
Bush lawyer *(Rubus schmidelioides)*
Cabbage tree *(Cordyline australis)*
Celery pine *(Phyllocladus alpinus)*
Chain fern *(Tmesipteris elongata)*
Club moss *(Lycopodium scariosum)*
Coprosma (various)
Creeping pratia *(Pratia angulata)*
Crown fern *(Blechnum discolor)*
Cup fungus *(Cyttaria gunnii)*
Cushion daisy *(Celmisia sessiflora)*
Cushion plant *(Phyllachne colensoi)*
Dagger leaf daisy *(Celmesia petriei)*
Easter orchid *(Earina autumnalis)*
Everlasting daisy
    (Helichrysum bellidioides)
Eyebright *(Euphrasia zealandica)*
Filmy fern
    (Hymenophyllum multifidum)
Fiordland spaniard
    (Aciphylla takahea)
Forstera sedifolia
Five finger *(Pseudopanax arboreus)*
Gentian *(Gentian montana)*
Giant moss
    (Dendroligotrichum dendroides)
Grass tree *(Dracophyllum fiordense)*
Haast's carrot *(Anistome haastii)*
Hanging spleenwort
    (Asplenium flaccidum)
Hen and chicken fern
    (Asplenium bulbi ferum)
Hooded orchid *(Pterostylis banksii)*

Hound's tongue fern
    (Phymatosorus diversifolius)
Kamahi *(Weinmannia racemosa)*
Kidney fern *(Cardiomanes reniforme)*
Kiokio *(Blechnum copense)*
Koromiko *(Hebe stricta)*
Ladies slipper orchid
    (Dendrobium cunninghamii)
Lancewood
    (Pseudopanax crassifolius)
Large flowered native broom
    (Carmichaelia grandiflora)
Large mountain daisy
    (Celmesia semicordata)
Maori onion
    (Bulbinella gibbsii)
Marble leaf *(Cardopetus serratus)*
Midribbed snow tussock
    (Chionochloa pallens)
Miro *(Podocarpus ferrugineus)*
Mistletoe *(Peraxilla tetrapetala)*
Mountain beech *(Nothofagus
    solandri* var. *cliffortioides)*
Mountain cabbage tree
    (Cordyline indivisa)
Mountain flax
    (Phormium cookianum)
Mountain holly *(Olearia ilicifolia)*
Mountain ribbonwood
    (Hoheria glabrata)
Mountain snowberry
    (Gaultheria depressa var. *novae-
    zealandiae)*
Mt Cook lily *(Ranunculus lyallii)*
Musky tree daisy *(Olearia moschata)*
New Zealand bluebell *(Wahlenbergia
    albomarginata)*

New Zealand violet
   (Viola cunninghamii)
Odd-leafed orchid
   (Aporostylis bifolia)
Palm leaf fern
   (Blechnum capense 'blackspot')
Pepper tree *(Pseudowintera colorata)*
Pineapple scrub
   (Dracophyllum menziesii)
Prickly shield fern
   (Polystichum vestitum)
Prince of Wales Feather fern
   (Leptopteris superba)
Rata *(Metrosideros umbellata)*
Red beech *(Nothofagus fusca)*
Rough tree fern
   (Dicksonia squarrosa)
Rimu *(Dacrydium cupressinium)*
Silver beech *(Nothofagus menziesii)*
Soft tree fern *(Cyathea smithii)*
Sundew *(Drosera arcturi)*

South Island edelweiss
   (Leucogenes grandiceps)
South Island mountain foxglove
   (Ourisia macrocarpa)
Sphagnum moss
   (Sphagnum cristatum)
Totara *(Podocarpus totara)*
Toetoe *(Cortaderia richardii)*
Turpentine scrub
   (Dracophyllum uniflorum)
Tutu *(Coriaria arborea)*
Tussock *(Chionochloa conspicua)*
Tree fuchsia *(Fuchsia excorticata)*
Whipcord hebe *(Hebe laingii)*
White rata *(Metrosideros diffusa)*
White snow marguerite
   (Senecio scorzoneroides)
Willowherb *(Epilobium glabellum)*
Wineberry *(Aristotelia serrata)*
Woolly head *(Craspedia uniflora)*
Vegetable sheep *(Raoulia eximia)*

Mt Cook lilies

Hound's tongue fern

Hybrid marguerite

Gentian

Kiokio (*Blechnum capense*)

Hooded orchid

Tree daisy

Eyebright

Native broom in flower

Celmesia

Edelweiss

Everlasting daisy

Easter orchid

13

BIRDS OF THE TRACK

Bellbird *(Anthornis melanura)*
Brown kiwi *(Apteryx australis)*
Black shag *(Phalacrocorax carbo)*
Blue duck
   (Hymenolaimus malacorphynchos)
Brown creeper
   (Finschia navaeseelandiae)
Canada goose *(Branta canadensis)*
Chaffinch *(Fringilla coelebs)*
Fiordland crested penguin
   (Eudyptes pachyrhynchus)
Fantail *(Rhipidura fuliginosa)*
Grey duck *(Anas superciliosa)*
Grey warbler *(Gerygone igata)*
Kaka *(Nestor meridionalis)*
Kea *(Nestor notabilis)*
Little shag
   (Phalacrocorax melanoleucos)
Long-tailed cuckoo
   (Eudynamis taitensis)

Morepork *(Ninox novaeseelandiae)*
New Zealand pigeon
   (Hemiphaga novaeseelandiae)
New Zealand scaup
   (Aythya novaeseelandiae)
Paradise shelduck
   (Tadorna variegata)
Pipit *(Anthus novaeseelandiae)*
Redpoll *(Carduelis flammea)*
Rifleman *(Acanthisitta chloris)*
Robin *(Petroica australis)*
Rock wren *(Xenicus gilviventris)*
Silvereye *(Zosterops lateralis)*
Tomtit *(Petroica macrocephala)*
Tui *(Prosthemadera novaeseelandiae)*
Yellow-crowned parakeet
   (Cyanoramphus auriceps)
Yellowhead *(Mohoua ochrocephala)*
Weka *(Galliralllus australis)*
White heron *(Egretta alba)*

Kea on southern rata

Tomtit

Robin

Rifleman

Pied fantail

Juvenile long-tailed cuckoo

Bellbird

Yellow-crowned parakeet

Tui

New Zealand pigeon

Blue duck

Female paradise shelduck

Brown kiwi

OBSERVATIONS

NAMES AND ADDRESSES

Name: . . . .
. . . .
Address: . . . .
. . . .
. . . .
Phone: . . . .

Name: . . . .
. . . .
Address: . . . .
. . . .
. . . .
Phone: . . . .

Name: . . . .
. . . .
Address: . . . .
. . . .
. . . .
Phone: . . . .

Name: . . . .
. . . .
Address: . . . .
. . . .
. . . .
Phone: . . . .

Name: . . . .
. . . .
Address: . . . .
. . . .
. . . .
Phone: . . . .

Name: . . . .
. . . .
Address: . . . .
. . . .
. . . .
Phone: . . . .

Name: . . . .
. . . .
Address: . . . .
. . . .
. . . .
Phone: . . . .

Name: . . . .
. . . .
Address: . . . .
. . . .
. . . .
Phone: . . . .

Name: . . . .
. . . .
Address: . . . .
. . . .
. . . .
Phone: . . . .

Name: . . . .
. . . .
Address: . . . .
. . . .
. . . .
Phone: . . . .